For Willie Llewellyn
K. W.

For Lotte Manning
M. M.

Text copyright © 1993 by Karen Wallace
Illustrations copyright © 1993 by Mick Manning

First U.S. edition 1993
Published in Great Britain in 1993
by Walker Books Ltd., London.

Library of Congress Cataloging-in-Publication Data:

Wallace, Karen.
Think of a beaver / Karen Wallace : illustrated by Mick
Manning. —1st U.S. ed.
Summary: Pictures and rhythmic text provide a close-up
look at the habits and homes of North American beavers.
1. Beavers—Juvenile literature. [1. Beavers.]
I. Manning, Mick, ill. II. Title. III. Series.
QL737. R632W35 1993
559.32'32—dc20   92-53132
ISBN 1-56402-179-3

10 9 8 7 6 5 4 3 2 1

Printed in Hong Kong

The pictures in this book are watercolor paintings.

Candlewick Press
2067 Massachusetts Avenue
Cambridge, Massachusetts 02140

THINK OF A BEAVER

Karen Wallace

illustrated by
Mick Manning

CANDLEWICK PRESS
CAMBRIDGE, MASSACHUSETTS

Think of a beaver.

The beavers in this book live in North America, but there are beavers in Europe and Asia as well.

Bright-eyed beaver, brown and bushy,

hurries to the stony lakeshore.

Beavers dam the stream with sticks, stones, roots and mud to make a pond.

Beaver breath is hot and woody—

he's grunting, puffing, dragging branches.

Beaver teeth

are sharp as chisels,

orange like

an autumn pumpkin.

Beavers eat lily roots.
They also eat bark and
young wood from aspen
and birch trees.

Beaver teeth

can cut through trees,

and grow again

when beaver breaks them.

Beaver hands
are monkey clever.
He builds a lodge
from mud and branches,
tunnels in
from underwater.

Beavers usually build their
lodge in the middle of the
pond. They leave spaces
in the roof to let in air.

Most beaver lodges have at least two tunnels.

A beaver can swim for a quarter of a mile without coming up for air.

Beaver feet are webbed
like ducks' feet,
push like paddles
through the water,
past the slowly
swimming salmon,
down to where
the tangled roots
lie buried in
the reedy lake bed.

Beaver feet are useful
for grooming, too.

Beavers live in families. Couples mate for life.

Beaver tail
is flat and scaly,
like a rudder
underwater,
like a trowel
for mud and branches,
carefully curled
and carried safely.

Beaver tail
sounds danger warning.
He whacks it *SLAP!*
upon the water.
Other beavers
hear the message...

Quickly dive!

Protect the young ones!

Find the tunnel

underwater!

Baby beavers are called kits.
A mother beaver usually
has two to four kits at a time.

Beaver kits are born
in May-time,
dry and warm
on wood-chip bedding.

They cry like children
when they're hungry.

They learn to swim
along the tunnel,
through the water
to the lodge roof.

They play like children
in the sunshine.

Brainy beaver, engineer now,
cuts canals through boggy meadows.

He chooses trees beyond the shore,

chops them down and floats them home.

Beaver couples work together.

When the days
are growing colder,
leaves are falling,
red and yellow,
busy beaver's
work is hardest.

He gathers wood
for winter eating,
for when the ice
is hard as iron.

He plasters mud
and sticks together,
mends his dam,
protects his shelter
against the cold
and snowy weather.

*Beavers greet each other
by chattering...*

*and nibbling each
other's cheeks.*

Bushy beaver's
warm in winter.
He doesn't mind
the icy water.

He grows two coats
to keep the cold out—
thick and silky
on the skin side,
rough and rainproof
on the outside.

All winter long,
while snow is falling,
when birds have flown
and bears are sleeping,
beaver lives
inside his lodge room,
warm and dry
on wood-chip bedding.
He nibbles at
his sunken branches,
combs his fur
and waits for spring.

Think of a beaver.